# THOSE DAYS IN JANUARY

# Those Days in January

## THE ABDUCTION AND MURDER OF MEREDITH HOPE EMERSON

John Cagle

**BOOK**LOGIX·
Alpharetta, GA

The author has tried to recreate events, locations, and conversations from his memories of them. The author has made every effort to give credit to the source of any images, quotes, or other material contained within and obtain permissions when feasible.

ISBN: 978-1-63183-732-6 - Paperback
eISBN: 978-1-63183-733-3 - ePub
eISBN: 978-1-63183-734-0 - mobi

Library of Congress Control Number: 2020900828

Printed in the United States of America            0 1 3 1 2 0

⊗This paper meets the requirements of ANSI/NISO Z39.48-1992 (Permanence of Paper)

*This book is dedicated to the hundreds of volunteers, dozens of emergency service workers and police officers, and the many friends of Meredith Emerson who searched for her during those days in January 2008;*

*and to criminal investigators across this country whose charge it is to investigate these horrific events and are forever changed by them. You're not alone.*

# TIMELINE

## December 31, 2007

**MIDMORNING** Gary Hilton arrives at the Blood Mountain approach trail parking lot.

**LATE EVENING** Meredith Emerson celebrates New Year's Eve with friends in Atlanta.

## January 1, 2008

**APPROXIMATELY 1:00 P.M.** Meredith Emerson arrives at the Blood Mountain approach trail parking lot with her dog, Ella.

**APPROXIMATELY 2:30 P.M.** Gary Hilton attacks and subdues Meredith Emerson on the trail.

**APPROXIMATELY 6:30 P.M.** Gary Hilton leaves the Blood Mountain approach trail parking lot with Meredith Emerson and Ella in his van.

**7:05 P.M.** Gary Hilton attempts to withdraw money using Emerson's ATM card at the Appalachian Bank in Blairsville, Georgia. Meredith Emerson provides an incorrect access code.

**9:00 P.M.** Gary Hilton attempts to withdraw money using Emerson's ATM card at the Bank of America in Gainesville, Georgia. Meredith Emerson provides an incorrect access code.

# January 2, 2008

**8:02 P.M.** Gary Hilton attempts to withdraw money using Emerson's ATM card at Regions Bank in Canton, Georgia. Meredith Emerson provides an incorrect access code.

# January 3, 2008

**4:35 P.M.** Gary Hilton calls former employer John Taber and requests money.

# January 4, 2008

**EARLY AFTERNOON** Meredith Emerson is murdered in Dawson Forest.

**4:00 P.M.** Meredith Emerson's dog Ella is recovered at the Kroger in Cumming, Georgia.

**4:41 P.M.** Gary Hilton calls Sean Stewart requesting money.

**APPROXIMATELY 6:45 P.M.** Meredith Emerson's identification and other evidence are recovered from dumpster at the QuikTrip in Cumming, Georgia.

**8:00 P.M.** Gary Hilton is arrested in Metro Atlanta.

# January 7, 2008

**4:00 P.M.** Gary Hilton discloses the location of the body of Meredith Emerson.

**7:00 P.M.** The body of Meredith Emerson is recovered from Dawson Forest.

# January 31, 2008

**2:00 P.M.** Gary Hilton is sentenced to life in prison for the murder of Meredith Emerson.

# INTRODUCTION

I was raised in a small mountain town in North Georgia. Kind of like Mayberry, where Andy and Barney took care of folks and things always seemed to work out at the end of the day. We didn't have a lot of crime, and when we did, the sheriff knew who to look for. Growing up, I can't remember having a murder or even a violent crime in my hometown. After stepping out of this sheltered life and getting into the world of law enforcement, I saw what can really happen. I was shocked, but as time passed, I thought I would get used to it. I was wrong.

This book describes the investigation of the abduction of Meredith Hope Emerson from a popular hiking trail in the mountains of North Georgia, only an hour's drive from my hometown. She was kept alive for four days before being brutally murdered. Her killer was also a suspect in two deaths in North Carolina and one in Florida. Following his arrest, he admitted he would have not stopped killing. Gary Michael Hilton hunted for victims in the National Forests of Georgia, North Carolina, and Florida, and is a true serial killer. He is pure evil.

Different from other true crime books, these events are told through the lens of the investigators. Some folks say justice rides a slow horse, but in January 2008, it didn't. Meredith Emerson was abducted on January 1, killed on January 4, and Gary Hilton was sentenced to life in prison on January 31. That is why this book may not be as lengthy as some others. But this story will last forever.

Meredith Emerson was the all-American girl, blessed with a wonderful family and group of friends. Her death changed their lives forever. These cases also affect those whose duty it is to investigate them.

Out of respect for the victims, you will not see crime-scene pictures. Learning how they died will be enough.

Working serious and sometime tragic investigations over three decades did not prepare me for the events that unfolded during those days in January. I retired from the Georgia Bureau of Investigation on April 1, 2008. This was my last case.

# 1

## SOMETHING BAD WILL HAPPEN HERE

*The Atlanta tract is bisected by Shoal Creek Road. There are several gated roads off to the west. They're not on the map. They're gated and the gates are closed, and they are designated as trails. I believe it's the first road to your left. A landmark for that would be the trail that has two blazes; one is lavender and the other gray. Go approximately forty yards.*

—Gary Michael Hilton

For those of us who grew up in small towns, life was different. Our parents never locked the doors of our house or cars. They let us walk or ride our bikes to school and other places around town without a worry. This was the way it was for me and my friends in Jasper, Georgia. Playing cops and robbers, mostly cops, filled the afternoons after elementary school, and sports and girls would take over later. Nevertheless, we were going to grow up and make a go of it in life doing something. We just didn't know what that something would be.

On June 3, 1972, my high school graduation ceremony took place at six p.m. I felt lucky, and a bit surprised that this night had come for me. You see, in my small hometown, graduating from high school was a big deal. For some, there were not a lot of opportunities to attend college, so many of my classmates chose to settle down in this small, North Georgia mountain town and live their lives. I was the last to walk across the platform and receive my diploma that night, simply because I was the tallest in my class. As I came down the steps leading from the platform, I wondered what was next. About a week later, a letter came informing me that I had been accepted to Western Carolina University. I was to report for orientation in early September.

Feeling somewhat intimidated that I was about to be a college man, I planned to throw away my high school bad habits of never studying, hunker down, and make the best of it. But before reporting to Western, I needed a summer job. Fortunately, a family friend had just gotten a contract to complete some demolition work in the next county over, and he hired me for the summer.

In the 1950s, a ten-thousand-acre tract of land near a town called Dawsonville became home to the Georgia Nuclear Aircraft Laboratory. The United States government purchased the land in order for the Air Force, Atomic Energy Commission, and Lockheed Aircraft Corporation to conduct research and develop a nuclear-powered aircraft. The facility consisted of a nuclear reactor site, a cooling site, and what was called a hot-cell building. Each site was connected by a railway system. There were also several metal buildings used for storage and office space, as well as an underground work area and parking deck. The nuclear reactor itself would be raised from its "storage pool" and hoisted into the open air when operational. When this occurred, massive doses of radiation were released into the surrounding area. After attempts to develop nuclear fuel for aircraft failed, other tests were performed at this site, such as studies to examine the effects of radiation on wildlife and vegetation. These tests were devastating to living things in the test area.

In 1971, the Department of Defense closed the facility, removed the reactor, and contracted for the remaining buildings and fencing to be removed. The City of Atlanta purchased the property and explored the idea of building a second airport. When that idea failed, they asked the Georgia Forestry Commission to manage it. The Dawson Forest Wildlife Management City of Atlanta Tract was later created on that site in 1975.

On the first day of my summer job, I was issued a radiation badge just in case I was exposed to high levels of radiation around the facility. If I received a dangerous amount of radiation, the color within the badge would change. Each week, I was issued a different badge.

The first area I worked in was just off a dirt road called Shoal Creek. I was joined by another boy near what looked to be several truckloads of dirt. For the first two weeks, we shoveled that dirt into iron containers that would be taken away to some storage facility in Alabama. Shoveling radioactive dirt was okay as long as the color on my badge remained the same. Finally, at the end of those two weeks, I took down fencing that had been in place for twenty years around the site.

The whole place was spooky, and after each workday ended, I would explore the other areas within the compound. The reactor site, which was mostly underground, was flooded. The vegetation for about two hundred yards around the site was dead. Small railroad tracks crisscrossed the compound on their way to the reactor, where railcars loaded with items to be irradiated would be delivered.

By the end of August 1972, my summer job was over. I was happy not to be shoveling radioactive dirt, wrestling with chain-link fencing, or wondering if my radiation badge would change. When I left, I hoped I would never come back. I had the feeling something bad would happen there. Little did I know, thirty-six years later, I would return on a cold night in January . . . when something did.

# 2

## A CAREER IN LAW ENFORCEMENT

*Reaching out to them gets their cooperation, because now you're making yourself a person to them instead of a monster. You're making them see you as just a guy who maybe has a screw loose.*

—Gary Michael Hilton

In June 1976, I graduated from college and began a career as a high school teacher in my hometown. You see, teaching runs in my family. My grandmother and mother were both teachers. I enjoyed teaching those first two years, and had the occasion to meet some special agents with the Georgia Bureau of Investigation who came to the school for Law Enforcement Appreciation Day. I listened as the agents told students all about the GBI. I think I was perhaps the most interested. The excitement of a stakeout, solving crimes and making arrests, took me back to the old cops-and-robbers games my friends and I played after school when we were growing up. But this was real.

In August 1979, I put my teaching days behind me and began working for the GBI. *What a job*, I thought. It was fun, but dangerous at times. However, I knew I had found what I wanted to do. Making the transition from high school teacher to GBI agent was a bit of a stretch—keeping the peace on the streets would be different from keeping the peace in the classroom. But there was no turning back. Having no prior law-enforcement experience meant I had to learn everything from the ground up. Instead of being the teacher, I was the student again.

After about three weeks of reading policies and having equipment issued to me, training began. I, along with about fifteen other agents, learned how to work undercover buying street-level amounts of drugs. Yes, my first assignment was as part of an undercover drug unit. The initial training lasted another three weeks, the third of which was spent at the firing range. I don't think I had ever fired a handgun before. But after firing several hundred rounds from my issued revolver (standard issue back then), I became proficient.

Once I hit the street, I was teamed up with an experienced partner who continued my training. This unit was organized with teams of two agents, who would travel to an area in the state that had been identified as having a drug problem. We would stay out of town for at least two weeks trying to infiltrate the local drug dealers. Once we had succeeded in doing so, we would return to headquarters, take our drug evidence to the state crime lab, turn in our paperwork, and take about four days off. Then we would repeat until the investigation was concluded.

Marty Zon was my training partner for the first trip out of town. He and I would spend each night going from bar to bar trying to engage someone in conversation, hoping to buy drugs from them. For six months, we worked in a college town in South Georgia. Marty was a good teacher, and I learned quickly. It was not long after that first investigation before I became a training partner.

In the fall of 1980, I was assigned to a fugitive squad in Atlanta. This unit, much like the current US Marshals Fugitive Task Force, looked for the worst of the worst fugitives. After coming off nothing but undercover assignments, it was now time to learn the fugitive business. Hunting people can be a huge challenge. Unlike hunting animals, these characters tend to fight back. I spent the next year in the most unsavory parts of Atlanta talking to prostitutes for information about where the bad guys were hiding. All of this was as new to me as the undercover unit had been the year before. I learned to predict what people on the run might do. Who they would contact or try to see. How we might set the trap and catch them. Most folks would reach out to a friend or relative for help, others to a prostitute or drug dealer. That's where we would be. GBI Special Agent Bruce Pickett taught me how to look for fugitives and how to stay alive doing it.

In the fall of 1981, I got the news I was being transferred to an investigative field office in North Georgia, where I would be assigned to what I call general crime. That means robberies, burglaries, murders, and occasionally more drug crimes. I was pleased to return to my hometown and begin that phase of my career.

As the years passed, I would again spend time in drug units. I was able to travel a lot this time while working major cases. I thought I wanted to work with the DEA and FBI on high-level drug investigations, and I had even considered applying for a job with them. But I decided against it for fear I might have to live and work in some ungodly place like Newark, New Jersey. Instead, I would stay in Georgia doing what I enjoyed.

The years went by quickly. I spent the majority of my GBI career working in the mountains of North Georgia, but now, the retirement years were getting closer. I had risen through the lowest levels of the GBI ranks to become Special Agent in Charge of a field investigative office—the same one I had been transferred to in 1981. Most consider the SAC of a field office to be the last word for criminal investigations in that region of the state. I had "grown up" in law enforcement with most of the local sheriffs and police officers in my region, so working with them was easy. Of course, from time to time there would be disagreements, usually over the political nature of some investigations, but we worked things out. It's amazing how something as simple as a voting booth can influence decisions sometimes.

I felt pleased and lucky one morning in June 2007 as I reflected on several high-profile cases my office had worked recently. The murder of a young mother by her husband had taken six months to solve. And then the arrest of a sheriff and his chief deputy, whom I had known for years and worked cases with in the past, had rounded out the year. Those cases had caught the attention of the Atlanta television market and the governor's office. We were able to prevail with successful prosecutions, and now things were slowing down.

I hung up the phone that morning after talking with the director of GBI human resources. I had called to ask for a projection for my retirement date. In order to receive full pension benefits, I would need to work until the end of March 2008. Yes, my first day of retirement was projected to be April Fools' Day 2008. Later that week, we had our monthly office meeting to discuss active investigations and other things going on. I told the agents and support staff of my projected "out date" and expressed the desire for a smooth ride until then. In other words, I hoped there would be no more high-profile cases, no more television reporters, and certainly no more calls from the governor's office for updates on cases.

Later that summer, things did slow down. You see, slow times in investigative offices are times to catch up on things in other cases. Also, agents are able to take time off with their families, not having to worry about being needed at the office. There's no predicting when crimes will occur, but it seemed, at least in my office, slow times would end very quickly. So we learned to take advantage of the downtime.

Fall in North Georgia is a special time. Long about mid-October, the leaves begin to change, the afternoons and nights cool down, and community festivals occur almost every weekend. The Marble Festival in one county showcases some of Georgia's marble mines. The marble used on the Lincoln Memorial and twenty-four columns on the east front of the US Capitol Building came from these mines. Another festival, in a town considered to be the apple capital of Georgia, draws thousands of people over a single weekend as vendors display crafts and even local folk art. And then there is the Moonshine Festival. This town, believed by some to be the birthplace of NASCAR, is centered around moonshiners who learned to drive fast to avoid revenuers. The antique car show is the best part of this one. All the festivals tend to wind down just in time for Thanksgiving.

I live in a cabin atop the North Georgia mountains, and for me, a fire in my wood heater marks the beginning of fall. That year, October was bringing out the full color of the leaves as they slowly dropped from their trees. Winter was close.

My hope for a low-profile ending to my career was in sight.

# 3

*The Blood Mountain trail is a good place to hunt because
it's the most used hiking trail in Georgia. It's a three-
and-a-half mile hike up 1,400 feet, and I'm amazed at
the number of people that do it. But see, it's a good place
to hunt in that you have a huge selection. But it's a bad
place to hunt because . . . too many witnesses.*

—Gary Michael Hilton

**M**eredith Emerson and her roommate, Julia Karrenbauer, lived in an apartment in a town called Buford, just north of Atlanta. Meredith, her boyfriend Steve Segars, and several of their friends had gone out partying on that last night of December 2007. After several hours, Meredith, in an effort to miss the post-party traffic, went home a little before midnight. She and Steve made plans to hang out on New Year's Day.

Meredith Emerson was twenty-four years old and had graduated from the University of Georgia in Athens. She was from a town in Colorado about two hours from Denver called Longmont. She enjoyed skiing and hiking in the mountains where she grew up. While going to the University of Georgia, she would frequently see and spend time with longtime friends of her family Doug and Peggy Bailey. After graduation, Meredith started a career in marketing and worked not too far from her apartment. She achieved a blue belt in judo and was good at it. She also took the time to adopt and train a black Labrador puppy, named Ella. Meredith was the all-American girl. She was the model most parents want their children to become. Smart, attractive, and eager to begin the next phase of her life.

January 1, 2008, was a good day to go hiking in the North Georgia mountains. Bright sunshine illuminated the mountaintops and provided warmth for hikers on the trail. I remember the temperature was in the midfifties that day, with what my father called a "Carolina-blue sky." It was a bit unusual for the weather to be that good in January.

At about daybreak, hikers began to arrive in the parking lot of the Byron Herbert Reece Memorial Trail. This trail exits the parking lot next to a kiosk that gives hikers information about the trail. The approach trail ascends Blood Mountain through a series of switchbacks and intersects with the Appalachian Trail after several miles. It is probably the most popular hiking destination in Georgia.

Steve Segars talked with Meredith on the phone at about eleven a.m. She had just gotten up and needed to take Ella for a walk. They had plans to spend New Year's Day together, but he had been "terse and short" with her on the phone. Shortly after this phone call, Meredith wrote a note to her roommate, Julia: "Gone hiking, took Ella, hope you had fun." It was not unusual for Meredith to go hiking, and Julia assumed she and Steve were together.

At 11:10 a.m., Bill Clawson arrived at the approach trail. He encountered several hikers on his way up the mountain. Meredith Emerson arrived in the parking lot of the approach trail with Ella just after noon. It was going to be a good day to hike with Ella, and they, too, started up the trail.

Clawson saw Meredith on his hike and described her as wearing a lavender zippered jacket and black exercise pants. On his way back down the mountain, Clawson saw an individual walking with Meredith and Ella. He noticed at a switchback that the trail had been disturbed on the slope of the hill. This was a violation of trail protocol, as it damages the environment near the trail. He then saw a man carrying a bag with two water bottles, doggy treats, a silver hair barrette, sunglasses, and a police baton. This man, later identified as Seth Blankenship, said he had found them on the ground just off the trail. Clawson continued his descent, and at one point, he stopped to catch his breath and caught movement out of the corner of his eye. The same man he had seen walking with Meredith earlier was watching him. He was making an effort not to be seen, so Clawson thought perhaps he was using the bathroom. The man turned and walked away into the forest. Once he reached the parking lot, Clawson talked to Seth Blankenship again about the items Blankenship found and the strange man seen with Meredith. Blankenship mentioned that when he had first seen this man, he had been wearing the police baton. Clawson decided to turn the items in at a small hiking store just up the road.

At about one o'clock that afternoon, Steve Segars called Meredith to apologize for how he'd spoken to her on their previous call. His call went straight to voicemail.

By late in the afternoon, the weather had changed. A cold front was approaching and the temperature dropping. At dusk, it began to snow and the winds picked up. By midnight on Blood Mountain, the temperature had dropped below zero and snow was accumulating.

# 4

*I got her around to the tree, but she wasn't yelling anymore. I said, "Honey, don't worry I've got your pin number and card. If I was going to hurt you, I'd hurt you." We had to go through some really thick stuff, cross a really steep ravine, a drainage ditch and stream at the bottom. And then cross country straight down to the parking lot. I put a little line around her neck just like a leash and that's the only way she was secured.*

—Gary Michael Hilton

O
n the morning of January 2, Julia realized Meredith had not come home. She tried to call Steve, but couldn't reach him. Even so, she was not that alarmed—until Meredith's boss called and reported that Meredith had not shown up at work. Julia notified Meredith's parents, and later that morning the family friend, Peggy Bailey, reported Meredith missing to local law enforcement.

Julia went home and searched through the apartment for any clues as to where Meredith had gone hiking New Year's Day. She found several places highlighted in various hiking guides. She and several of Meredith's friends split up and headed to the mountains in hopes of finding Meredith.

The drive up the mountain was difficult that afternoon. The temperature was in the single digits, and ice and frozen snow became heavier at the mountaintop. Julia and her friends arrived at the approach trail late that afternoon. She immediately discovered Meredith's car in the parking lot, covered with snow. They all rushed up the trail looking for Meredith. Having no luck locating her, they called law enforcement and emergency services, who were familiar with the trail, as they had looked for overdue hikers in the past. The US Forest Service rangers were also notified, because Blood Mountain is situated in the Chattahoochee National Forest. Realizing that conditions were worsening, and knowing the dangers of deploying a search party in the dark, plans were made to meet early the next morning to continue the search. But the question remained: could someone who was lost or possibly injured survive on the mountain in that kind of weather?

That night, my cell phone rang. It was Clay Bridges, an agent in my office. That usually meant something had happened in our territory and local law enforcement was asking for assistance. Clay was assigned to our northern counties, which included the area surrounding the National Forest. Our office enjoyed a good relationship with local law enforcement in these areas. I listened to Clay's report: a request made regarding a missing hiker on Blood Mountain. Missing hikers were not something we routinely became involved with, but the trigger prompting the request had been the discovery of Meredith's belongings on the approach trail. Some of the items were puzzling. Why would she leave her water bottles and Ella's dog treats on the trail?

But the discovery of the police baton was extremely concerning. Although these can be easily obtained by civilians, it's rare to see them on trails. Pepper spray, maybe, but what is essentially an extendable lead pipe had to be a first.

# 5

*There comes a point when they fight and then they submit, and a lot of that is because of me. I reassure them. I reassure them that it is going to be okay.*

—Gary Michael Hilton

As I was driving to the office the next morning, I heard the news reports about the missing hiker on Blood Mountain. Search efforts had begun late the previous afternoon, but had been called off after sunset. I contacted my agents and instructed them to meet me early that morning to be briefed by Clay Bridges and discuss a strategy. By 8:30 a.m., all the agents had arrived and we prepared, as best we could, to begin the investigation.

A decision had been made to close the Blood Mountain approach trail and parking lot. We also established the command center for the search effort at a nearby state park about a mile down the mountain. Established in 1931, Vogel State Park is the second oldest in Georgia. It is located at the base of Blood Mountain in the Chattahoochee National Forest and consists of the usual cabins and campsites. A twenty-two-acre lake is open to visitors in the summer. Many of its facilities were constructed by the Civilian Conservation Corps during the Great Depression. I had camped there as a young boy with my family and remembered it well. Now it would serve as our home for the next several days.

Before we left the office for Blood Mountain, we received an update on the search effort. It appeared several hundred volunteers were showing up at Vogel to help with the search. The hiking community, it seemed, is a close-knit group. Especially Appalachian Trail hikers—they have their own network to communicate on and off the trail. And word had gone out the night before to meet at Vogel and begin the search for Meredith.

I arrived at the park at about 10:00 a.m. and met with the local sheriff and the director of emergency management for Union County. The temperature that morning was in the single digits, but the sun was brightly shining. At the park, there was a main office used by the ranger and a fairly large building that housed the museum. In this museum were artifacts found at or near the site when the park was constructed. It was basically one large room. We agreed that the EMS director would lead the search effort and set up his command post in that museum. We would supplement him by assigning a police officer or agent with each search party. Our command post would be in a cabin nearby.

The satellite trucks were beginning to arrive in the parking lot and reporters were searching for someone to interview. I recognized a few from past investigations, but I was hesitant to engage them until I could get a handle on things. As more of my agents arrived, we knew we needed to establish a "tip line" so we could receive information from the public. There was only one real telephone at the park, in addition to one pay phone, so establishing the tip line there was out of the question. The sheriff and I decided to set it up at his office twelve miles away.

These days, the telephone systems of government agencies tend to have automated instructions. You know, press one for English and so forth. This tip line had to be answered immediately by a human. In these kinds of events, some people struggle with reporting information. They just don't want to get involved. Unfortunately, some are looking for any reason not to call. When they hear an automated message, they will hang up and simply say, "I tried." So we decided to ask the telephone company to install a bank of phones so we could staff the tip line with GBI agents. They would then relay information to us on our cell phones at the park. Jesse Maddox, the assistant special agent in my office, was in charge of the tip line. I asked for support from other work units in order to man the tip line twenty-four hours a day.

At about noon, I was notified that the GBI director and the bureau's public information officer were on their way to Vogel. Though Vernon Keenan had worked his way through the ranks to become director, he was an investigator trapped in a director's body. He loved to get involved with investigations and support his agents. Some supervisors were intimidated by Vernon and dreaded him showing up at scenes. But in the past couple of years, my office had been involved in high-profile cases, so Vernon knew what to expect from my agents and me. Plus, our PIO, John Bankhead, could take the pressure off me with the media.

With our command post/cabin up and running, the agents went to work. Clay contacted Wachovia and placed emergency tracking on all bank accounts pertaining to Meredith Emerson. The loss-management investigator told Clay he would alert him directly if any activity was noted on Emerson's accounts. Clay asked specifically if there had been any activity since December 31, 2007. The investigator reported there had not been any activity. Those reports would later turn out to be wrong. But we do reports every time we talk to folks, you know. And we had them.

We also contacted Verizon Wireless pertaining to her cell phone. They confirmed that the last telephone call placed from her phone was to her boyfriend on January 1, 2008, at approximately 11:00 a.m. The last telephone call to her phone was at 2:40 p.m. According to Verizon, Emerson's phone had been cut off between those two times and remained off now.

At noon, the Atlanta news crews were live on location for the noon news broadcast. The reports included photographs of Meredith and basic information about her, as well as our tip line telephone number. We were asking for anyone with information about her whereabouts or who had seen her on the Blood Mountain trail New Year's Day to call. We immediately began to receive information from several people who had seen her hiking up the approach trail to the summit. We also began to get information about a strange man with a tan dog who had been on the trail near Meredith at various points.

At 2:09 p.m., Jesse Maddox received a call from a person who stated he thought he knew the man described as being on the trail with Meredith. The caller, John Taber, said he had at one time employed a man named Gary Michael Hilton. He had known Hilton for approximately ten years and recognized his physical description from the noon press release. He also recognized the description of Hilton's dog, Dandy. He gave Jesse information about Hilton's 2001 Chevrolet Astro van and provided the tag number. According to Taber, Hilton frequently traveled to Blood Mountain and other state and national parks to camp and hike. Hilton was also known to carry a variety of weapons, including police batons. Before ending the call, he supplied Jesse with Hilton's identifying information (date of birth, Social Security number, etc.).

By 2:30 p.m., we sent the television channels a photograph of Gary Hilton and requested that anyone who knew him or had known him to call the tip line.

Late that afternoon, Meredith's parents, Susan and Dave Emerson, arrived at Vogel State Park. Peggy Bailey and her husband were with them. We got them a cabin next to our command post. The sheriff and I introduced ourselves and briefed them on our progress.

Those of us in this business have a hard, fast rule: we don't disclose details about ongoing investigations to the media or to friends or family. It's not that we believe information will be leaked with bad intent. However, it's important that any strategy we have or develop is known only to the investigators, so as not to jeopardize the outcome. I had just gone through this in another high-profile investigation when the father of a missing woman had appeared on "talking-head" television shows demanding an arrest in the case. Had I disclosed any information to the father during that investigation, I knew I would see it on television. The investigation, ultimately, had been successful—because we kept quiet.

However, after I met Susan and Dave Emerson, and Doug and Peggy Bailey, I threw the rules out the window. These were good and decent people, and they needed to know the truth. I could see the horror and worry in their eyes. Even though it wouldn't be what they wanted to hear, I had to tell them everything. So that afternoon, we sat down and I told them what was being done, and that we hoped it was not as bad as it seemed.

As the afternoon progressed, search teams struck out into the forest and backroads of Blood Mountain. We were joined by many other police agencies. Helicopters flew overhead and more satellite trucks from the news media filled the parking lot. Information poured into the tip line from more hikers who had seen Meredith and the strange man on the trail New Year's Day.

At about 6:30 p.m., Jesse Maddox wanted to clarify some information he had received from John Taber, Hilton's former employer, earlier in the day. Jesse called him and learned that at about 4:30 that afternoon, Hilton had called Taber asking for money. The first call was placed from telephone number 770-893-9922, but because of a bad connection, a second call was placed at 4:40 from telephone number 770-894-4684. Hilton stated that he had gotten his life in order and wanted to come back to work. He would need about $700 to get his driver's license and tags renewed. He asked that a check be left at the business in Atlanta so he could pick it up.

This was a major setback for the investigation because of the lag time between the conversation at 4:40 p.m. and the 6:30 p.m. call from Jesse. Taber later would say that following the phone call with Hilton, he had gone into a business meeting, and had he known Hilton had a hostage, he would have called then. However, that story does not hold water. There was never a moment during a single media release that did not mention Meredith Emerson.

One of the telephone numbers Hilton used to call was determined to be from a Huddle House located at 35 Foothills Parkway, Marble Hill, Georgia—sixty miles southwest of Blood Mountain. The other number was a pay phone next door to the Huddle House.

At 9:15 p.m., I arrived at the Huddle House in Marble Hill. This was only a few miles from my cabin, and I knew the area well. It was a stone's throw from the Dawson Forest Wildlife Management Area where I had worked during the summer of '72. The cook remembered seeing Gary Hilton come in to have a cup of coffee. He had been wearing a fur-lined flap hat, a green jacket, and cargo pants. He asked to make a phone call from the house phone on the counter. According to the cook, the phone call had lasted a couple of minutes.

A store next to the Huddle House had a pay phone. The manager stated she had seen a white Chevrolet Astro parked outside the store that afternoon. The number was confirmed to be the first number that had called John Taber.

The DeKalb Police Department SWAT team was asked to watch Taber's business in Atlanta, and if Hilton showed up, they were told to grab him and immediately search his van for Meredith. But he never showed up.

As darkness fell at Vogel State Park and the searches concluded for the night, the volunteers, now numbering in the hundreds, were provided hot meals by local church groups and other volunteers. The information coming to us from many sources throughout the day had not been good. You see, the longer these things go on, the less likely they are to result in a good outcome. And a clearer picture of Gary Hilton and his profile was emerging: dangerous and unpredictable. Park rangers remembered coming upon him at various locations in the National Forest and described his bizarre and at times confrontational behavior.

I only slept about an hour that night worrying about Meredith. If she was in the company of someone like Gary Hilton, what would come next? She had to be cold and scared and concerned for herself and Ella. I was also worried she might have been injured during an attack. I ran through almost every scenario that night, and none of them were good.

# 6

## PROFILE OF
## A SERIAL KILLER

*I was really a pathetic guy in that, you see, the saddest thing in the world is a loner, which I was . . . a loner trying not to be one.*

—Gary Michael Hilton

ollowing interviews with witnesses who saw Meredith on the trail New Year's Day and interacted with whom we now believed was Gary Hilton, we began to learn more about him. Several rangers remembered seeing him in the past, camping in the forest near Blood Mountain. His sometimes aggressive behavior had made an impression on them. John Taber's work experience with him confirmed how unstable he had been years before. Our background investigation revealed the following:

> Gary Hilton was born on November 22, 1946. His father served in the medical corps of the United States Army. When his parents divorced, he and his mother moved to Florida. There, at eight years old, his mother sent him to a "boys' club," where he did well. His mother remarried when Hilton was nine, and he, his mother, and his stepfather would travel the country looking for work. His teachers would routinely tell his mother how well he was doing in school, and many of them felt he should be moved up a grade. However, tensions grew between Hilton and his stepfather, and when he was fourteen, they got into an argument. Hilton was upset about how his mother was being treated. He had borrowed a gun from a friend, and during the argument his stepfather said, "Just shoot me."

Hilton's stepfather survived the gunshot wound and Hilton was arrested.

Hilton entered the US Army at the age of seventeen, where he volunteered to become a paratrooper and later attended airborne school at Fort Benning, Georgia. His first assignment was in Germany. He later told his mother he was a Green Beret, but his military records do not reflect that.

After the army, Hilton attended school to become a pilot and a flight instructor. As time passed, he married a couple of times, but both marriages failed. He was arrested for minor offenses—theft and simple battery—and never served any lengthy time in jail.

I and other agents interviewed Gary Hilton over the course of our investigation. During these interviews, some lasting for hours, it became clear that his behavior was similar to that of other serial killers. His lack of remorse for his killings, his psychopathic ramblings, and his views about society and himself among the many.

Most serial killers are proud of their work. Gary Hilton was no exception.

# 7

*The evidence was good right out of the dumpster.*
*It was just a smoking gun; they had me.*

—Gary Michael Hilton

As the sun came up at Vogel State Park, the church groups and volunteers prepared breakfast for everyone. The skies were blue, but the temperature was still in the twenties. The tip line had been active all night, and calls continued to come in with reports of seeing Gary Hilton on the trail New Year's Eve and New Year's Day. I met with the Emersons to assure them that searches were continuing and a nationwide lookout had been placed on Gary Hilton. I updated the search team leaders with the latest information.

At about 11:00 a.m., an investigator with the Ducktown, Tennessee, sheriff's office came to our investigative command post and asked me if we were aware of an active investigation in North Carolina concerning the murder of an elderly female and the disappearance of her husband near a hiking trail in the Pisgah National Forest. He also said there was another investigation in Florida regarding the murder of a woman in a National Forest down there. As a result of his information, we learned the following:

On October 21, 2007, John and Irene Bryant, both in their eighties, had decided to go for a day hike in the Pisgah National Forest. John is what is called a "through hiker," meaning he had hiked the entire distance of the Appalachian Trail. They parked their car on a forest service road that day to begin their hike. Later, a 911 call was attempted from their cell phone, but the call had been dropped because of a weak signal.

Irene's sister was in the habit of calling often, but had not been able to reach Irene in over a week. Their son, who lived in Austin, Texas, decided to come to Hendersonville and check on his parents. He got to their home, and while everything appeared to be normal, their packs were gone. He assumed they had gone hiking, and notified authorities that his parents were missing. The search for John and Irene began.

The following day, their car was found parked at a trailhead in the forest. Officials learned someone had used the couple's bank card on October 22, 7:35 p.m., to withdraw $300 from the Peoples Bank in Ducktown, Tennessee, two hours away. Security cameras showed a person wearing a mask walk up to the ATM.

It was not long before the body of Irene Bryant was discovered. Her cause of death was blunt-force trauma to the head. John Bryant remained missing. Despite an intensive search and investigation by the Transylvania County Sheriff's Office, the US Forest Service, and the FBI, there were no clues of his whereabouts. The case went cold.

Less than two months later, on December 1, Cheryl Hodges Dunlap, forty-six, disappeared in the Apalachicola National Forest near Tallahassee, Florida. She was a nurse and mother of two grown children. She also taught Sunday school, and when she failed to arrive to class the next day, her friends became concerned. On December 3, when she failed to show up for work, she was reported missing to Leon County law enforcement. The next day, her car was discovered on a road near the entrance to the National Forest. The left rear tire appeared to have been punctured.

As is the case with most missing persons, Cheryl's bank account was flagged. Officers learned that on December 2, 3, and

4, her ATM card had been used at several local banks. The security footage showed a man wearing gloves, glasses, and what appeared to be a homemade mask. Officers staked out the banks, with no luck.

On December 8, almost two hundred people searched the wooded area close to where her car had been found, again with no luck.

On December 15, witnesses reported seeing buzzards circling in the forest. Officers determined through DNA analysis that it was the body of Cheryl Dunlap. Her head and hands were missing. A day later, witnesses reported seeing Gary Hilton camping on a pig trail in the forest off Joe Thomas Road.

On December 28, 12:47 p.m., a Forest Service ranger encountered Hilton in the Osceola National Forest, adjacent to the Apalachicola National Forest. He was issued a citation for camping in an unauthorized area and for driving on a closed road. He was instructed to leave. Camping in an unauthorized area in the forest seemed to be his MO, as that was the reason law enforcement had encountered him in the Georgia forests.

Later that day, we were contacted by the US Marshals Service, who had determined during a search of their database that Meredith Emerson's debit card had been used that week. This, of course, was not what Wachovia's investigators had been telling us. According to the marshals, at 7:05 p.m. on January 1, 2008, attempts had been made to withdraw money at the Appalachian Community Bank in Blairsville, Georgia, thirteen miles from the Blood Mountain approach trail. These were just attempts; no money was obtained. The wrong PIN number had been used.

Between 9:31 p.m. and 9:54 p.m., seven more attempts occurred at the Bank of America in Gainesville, Georgia, sixty miles south of the Blood Mountain approach trail. On January 2, another attempt was made at the Regions Bank in Canton, Georgia, eighty miles southwest of the trail. This could only mean that during that time, Meredith was still alive. I was horrified. She had been doing all she could to stall, giving Hilton the wrong PIN number in the hope that we would catch up. She must have realized he would have no more use for her if she gave him the correct access code.

At about four o'clock that afternoon, a call came to the tip line from a woman who said she had been following the news coverage and thought she had just seen Meredith's dog, Ella. She was in a Kroger grocery store in Cumming, Georgia (seventy miles south of the trail), and a dog had walked into the store. She was able to catch the dog in the parking lot and asked us what to do. At 6:05 p.m. it was confirmed, using an identification chip, that the dog was Ella. Now we were getting somewhere. Could Meredith be close by too? But as soon as the call about Ella had come, the area was flooded with police officers. No sign of Gary Hilton or his van. He was gone.

At 6:10, only five minutes after we knew we had Ella, Sean Stewart called the tip line and reported the following. She had known Gary Hilton for about twenty to thirty years and had just received a call from him asking for money. She told him, "Don't you know the world is looking for you?" He hung up. She gave us the number that had appeared on her caller ID, which we quickly determined was from a pay phone at a QuikTrip service station across the street from the Kroger Ella had walked into. Both were eighty miles south of the trail. As you might imagine, there were soon a number of patrol cars headed to the QuikTrip.

The pay phone was on the outside wall of the storefront, and the number on the phone was confirmed to be the one that had earlier called Sean Stewart. The employees were interviewed, and they identified Gary Hilton as the man who had used the telephone. They also said he had been cleaning out his van and throwing things into the dumpster next to the store. Because it seemed he was headed south, the Metro Atlanta police departments were notified to be on the lookout again for Hilton's van. Special Agent Mitchell Posey arrived at the QuikTrip and began to process the scene.

Shortly before 8:00 p.m., a call was placed to the DeKalb 911 center reporting a person at a car wash cleaning out a white van. The caller thought it was the person being looked for regarding the disappearance of the hiker on the Blood Mountain trail. The 911 operator told him she was dispatching units to that location. The caller said, "I can grab him for you if you want me to."

Just after that, he reported police officers had arrived and the person was in custody. I was immediately in touch with the officers at the scene, who informed me that Meredith was not in the van. *Damn.* Three GBI agents from the investigative team arrived shortly after the arrest. Hilton was calm and collected, but not cooperative. They took him to our Atlanta office, where he proceeded to recite the Miranda warnings before they even had the chance to.

Back at the QuikTrip, crime-scene processing continued. The dumpster was located in the north end of the parking lot, where it was dimly lit by the streetlight. Inside were the things I had hoped we wouldn't find. In a white garbage bag was a black, leather women's wallet containing Meredith Emerson's driver's license. Several other pieces of paperwork bearing her name were found throughout the bag as well. A second white garbage bag revealed a fleece pullover covered with dirt, hair, and vegetation debris. On the fleece was a red substance that tested positive for blood. A blue sweatshirt held more debris, with leaves reddened by a wet substance that also tested positive for blood. Another sweatshirt was saturated in blood. We also found a US Forest Service warning citation issued on December 28, 2007, at 12:45 p.m. to Gary M. Hilton. The warning had been issued to Hilton in the National Forest in Florida for driving on a closed road and camping in an unauthorized place. There was blood on the ticket. An

Atlanta newspaper, dated January 4, 2007, was also in the dumpster, along with metal chains and bloodstained nylon rope.

By now it was after midnight, and as I made my way to my cabin to try to get some sleep, I thought about the briefing with the Emersons that would take place in a few hours. We had the man we had been looking for all week, but we didn't have Meredith. At this point, I felt there was very little chance of finding her alive. I knew her parents would feel the same way. The air was about to be sucked out of the search teams and volunteers at Vogel who were working so hard to find her. We had to bring them closure. Instead of search and rescue, it was now search and recover.

# 8

*Listen, the reason for killing the girl . . . once you've taken someone, you're either going to kill them or you're just going to get caught. It's as simple as that.*

—Gary Michael Hilton

I t was not yet daybreak as I began the hour-long drive to Vogel State Park. The command post had been notified of Hilton's arrest, and I wanted to meet with Meredith's parents to tell them before they heard it from anyone else.

I arrived just after sunup. The search teams were being organized and were about to leave the park. I traveled directly to the cabin where the Emersons were staying and updated them on the events of the previous day. Before I could continue, their expressions confirmed that they knew we did not have Meredith. But there was more I had to tell them. I will never forget the horror in their eyes as I explained the evidence we had recovered from the dumpster. They needed details, and I had to provide them: the bloodstained clothes, her driver's license and wallet, and the bloodstained chains and rope. Several minutes went by without anyone speaking. We were still hopeful somehow we would find Meredith unharmed wandering in the forest, I said. But deep down inside, I knew, and I believe they did also, that we would not.

A few minutes later, we were joined by one of the crime-scene specialists, who was there at my request to obtain buccal swabs (DNA samples) from the Emersons. We had to confirm that the blood recovered Friday night was Meredith's. I gave them an update on the areas we were searching and the ATM information.

At about 9:00 a.m., the waiting members of the media who had learned of Hilton's arrest the night before needed an update. We continued to ask them through their newscasts to ask people to call our tip line with any sightings of Hilton and his van. Now we had recent photographs to distribute. Clay Bridges obtained an arrest warrant for Gary Hilton, charging him with kidnapping with bodily harm. Hilton was now in the Union County jail.

As I was briefing the investigative team in our cabin, Jesse Maddox, the agent in charge of the tip line, came in and said a call had been received early that morning from a person who believed he had seen Hilton's van at about noon on Friday. He had been in the Dawson Forest Wildlife Management Area/City of Atlanta Tract looking for hunting locations. As he approached a road identified as Duck Pond Road, he saw a white Chevrolet Astro backed in next to a gate. There was no one in or around the van. He returned to his truck and tried to take a picture of the van, but his camera was dead. After retrieving fresh batteries from his house, he returned—but the van was gone. Search teams were immediately dispatched. This was seventy miles south of the approach trail. Agent Bobby McElwee found the area in Dawson Forest described by the caller. In the V of a small tree, he found some paper towels. Near the tree on the ground were some rawhide dog treats.

Since we now had Hilton, we were able to compare his actual size and build to the photos obtained from the various ATM attempted transactions in our case. The ATM transactions from the night of January 1 had produced images of a person trying to disguise himself with a bandana at the Appalachian bank in Union County. The size and build matched Hilton's. The cameras were not working at the Bank of America in Gainesville. The image captured at the Regions Bank in Canton on January 2 confirmed it was Hilton who had attempted the transaction. He was wearing the same cloths as when he was arrested the night before. These photos were certainly helpful in our case, but they could also help in the North Carolina and Florida cases. Any similarities in the clothing worn, his body build, and even the mask would work.

Gary Hilton's van had been taken to our main investigative office, where it was being searched and processed. After leaving the forest, Bobby returned to the office to look at the van. A roll of paper towels on the dashboard matched the design on the towels he had found earlier in the forest. There were also rawhide dog treats on the floor of the van. This confirmed for all of us that Bobby had discovered Gary Hilton's campsites. While searching the van, the investigators identified a reddish-brown stain on the passenger-side sliding door. A presumptive test was positive for blood. A paper towel with the same design as the others was found under the rear floor mat—also positive for blood. There was an area on the rear of the driver's seat consistent with the appearance of a blood hair transfer. Think what it might look like if someone dipped a loofah in paint and touched it to a wall. This, too, was positive for blood.

After an arrest is made in a significant case, an investigator's natural tendency is to relax a bit. We could not; we didn't have Meredith. At Vogel, several of us, along with the GBI director, were discussing what would come next. How long should we keep searching Blood Mountain after learning about the Dawson Forest discovery? I made a statement that seemed to shock some folks: "We have to get this man a lawyer."

I was actually considering telling a lawyer everything about an active investigation. Usually we are not in the business of providing lawyers to suspects, but Gary Hilton knew where Meredith was. He was the only one. I telephoned the prosecutor who would handle the case in Union County and told him the same thing. At first his response was, "Let's see if he qualifies for a court-appointed lawyer."

"What are you talking about?" I said. "He lives in a van in the forest, so I think he qualifies."

He said he would get back to me.

I met with the search team leaders as they returned to Vogel that night, where I briefed them on the latest news from Dawson Forest. Many volunteers were still there, but they would have to leave soon and get back to their normal lives. The holiday week was coming to an end. The Emersons would leave soon, too, since we were scaling back the search effort at Vogel. They would be staying with Doug and Peggy Bailey in Athens. Additional resources were going to be sent to Dawson Forest the next morning, and activities on Blood Mountain would end. The tip line was still receiving calls, but not as many as before. A few more came in confirming sightings of Hilton in Dawson Forest.

Ella was brought to Vogel and reunited with Meredith's parents. Dave Emerson passed along some information he had received from a psychic earlier in the afternoon. In times like these, families are hungry for help, and often are referred to psychics by someone who has had experience with them in the past. Also, in high-profile cases like this, psychics will reach out directly to investigators and family members. In a few cases in the past, I received information from psychics but never put much stock in it. One called the office a couple years back to tell me where the body of another missing girl would be found. When pressed, he admitted he had never been in Georgia but had looked at a map and somehow come up with the location. We found the girl buried in a shallow grave nowhere near the psychic's description.

This one was in New York and had told Dave that Meredith would be found near railroad tracks. One thing was for sure: there were no railroad tracks near Blood Mountain.

# 9

*I didn't kill them for any satisfaction.*
*It was distasteful; it was dreadful.*

—Gary Michael Hilton

One more day would be spent searching in the mountains, and then the search there would be suspended. I had developed a routine and as usual briefed the search teams and media on the investigation. The church groups continued to provide hot meals to everyone. Over the last few days, it seemed many of us had gotten to know each other pretty well. But the looks on everyone's faces that day were of disappointment. Additional search teams were being sent to help Bobby in Dawson Forest, including dog teams and helicopters. Volunteers who had been camping in tents were packing up. The weather was warming as Sunday went by.

At about ten o'clock, I got a call from the prosecutor confirming that the public defender's office would be representing Gary Hilton. They were going to talk to him later that morning. We still had no leads on Meredith's location, so I was about to break an important rule during criminal investigations. I was going to tell Hilton's lawyers everything. The ATM transaction attempts and the images we had. What we found in the dumpster at QuikTrip. I was going to tell them everything because I wanted to know where Meredith Emerson was. The only person who knew was Gary Hilton, and he had lawyered up. At about noon, I met with the public defender and his investigator at the jail where Hilton was being housed. I arranged for them to bring him to a private office just outside the inner workings of the jail. And they began to talk.

Meanwhile, Bobby McElwee held a briefing in Dawson Forest with the additional search teams. As they began searching an area near the Etowah River, searchers found duct tape and cellophane wrappings along the riverbank. The duct tape appeared to be in good condition, which led Bobby to conclude it had only been there a short period of time. Helicopters arrived to help with the search, and Bobby assigned a ranger from the Department of Natural Resources as the spotter. The ranger, William Thacker, had worked for DNR many years and was probably more familiar with Dawson Forest than anyone. Over the years, he had worked to build the roads and trails, and managed the forest during hunting season. If Meredith was there, he would find her. I had met William one summer when I was home from college, and we had both worked as lifeguards at a resort, where we became close friends. Our paths had crossed over the years, and we always remembered that summer working together. He was a trusted friend, and like me was soon to retire. He was the kind of person who could be depended on in the most difficult situations. And this was one of them.

I sat in the hallway outside the office where Hilton was being interviewed by his lawyer. It was an unsecured area of the jail, and I was not willing to risk losing Hilton. Seconds turned into minutes, and minutes to hours. I could hear them talking, but I couldn't understand what they were saying. At one point, the investigator opened the door of the office and came out into the hallway where I was leaning up against the wall in my chair. I think initially he thought I was trying to eavesdrop on their conversation, but as he stood there, he could only hear voices, not words.

Hours later, their interview was finally over and Gary Hilton was returned to his jail cell. I met with his lawyer and investigator outside. "Where is Meredith Emerson?" I asked them. They asked if I would call the prosecutor and discuss whether the death penalty could be taken off the table in return for Meredith. I made the call immediately.

I am very much in favor of the death penalty, and if there was ever a likely candidate, it was Gary Hilton. But closure for Meredith Emerson's family and friends had to be considered. Ultimately, I recommended the swap, and the prosecutor agreed. I returned to the public defender with my answer. To my dismay, he said he wanted Hilton to "sleep on it." I was livid. But if it worked, what was a few more hours?

As I was walking out of the Union County jail, a guy walked up to me claiming to be the lawyer representing Gary Hilton. He introduced himself as Samuel Rael. He had defended Hilton on several charges over the years, including arson and false solicitation of charitable donations, and now he wanted to speak with me. In 1995, Rael had decided he wanted to make movies, and his friend and client Gary Hilton had plenty of ideas. Hilton acted as consultant while making the movie *Deadly Run*. His suggestion was to have a beautiful woman out in the woods, who would then be hunted down like prey. He found shooting locations in the North Georgia mountains near a town called Cleveland about twenty miles south of Blood Mountain. In the movie, the killer held women captive in a cabin and then released them into the forest to be hunted and killed. Rael admitted what Hilton had come up with back then was almost word for word what had happened now. He wanted to ask Hilton to cooperate with us.

If this case weren't bizarre enough, now enters some Atlanta lawyer turned Z-movie maker. I was not going to allow this character to complicate what I hoped would be a deal. Hilton had talked with his real attorneys for almost three hours, and this one could destroy any confidence he had in them. Maintaining silence was the last thing I wanted. I was now convinced that Meredith Emerson and Cheryl Dunlap had become part of Hilton's movie.

That afternoon, several crime-scene specialists continued to search and document the contents of Gary Hilton's van. Hundreds of items were being discovered and catalogued. I received a call from the director informing me that the law enforcement team and members of the United States Attorney's Office from North Carolina, who were investigating the murder of Irene Bryant and the disappearance of John, were coming for a briefing at my office on Monday. Members of the Leon County Sheriff's Office from Tallahassee would be there as well. I wanted to allow the crime-scene folks to brief the group about the evidence they found in the van. The FBI's Behavioral Science Unit was also coming. This was extremely rare, because unlike in *Criminal Minds* and other TV shows, investigators have to present cases to the BSU at their headquarters in Quantico, Virginia. They were definitely interested in Gary Michael Hilton.

The Dawson Forest search continued all afternoon, and the sheer size of the Atlanta tract and its difficult terrain became frustrating for the searchers. I talked with Bobby after he suspended the search that night, and we decided that we needed to devote all our resources there. The only thing that would remain active on Blood Mountain would be the tip line. That night, calls continued to come in with reports of a white van seen at more locations in Dawson Forest.

# 10

*I spent three days with her. We had long talks about everything. I gave her a book to read,* Cannibals and Kings.

—Gary Michael Hilton

The meeting to brief the other investigative teams was scheduled for ten o'clock Monday morning in the upstairs portion of our office. We had prepared a presentation that would allow others to see what evidence we recovered that might help in their investigations. At 9:30, investigators with the Transylvania County Sheriff's Office arrived, accompanied by FBI agents from Asheville, North Carolina, and representatives from the United States Attorney's Office for the Western District of North Carolina. By the start of the meeting, members of the Ducktown Sheriff's Office and the US Forest Service law enforcement division had also arrived.

I began with an overall briefing of our investigation and the arrest of Gary Hilton the previous Friday. The chief of our Division of Forensic Science, DNA section, confirmed to the group that the bloodstained clothing recovered from the dumpster at QuikTrip was confirmed to contain the blood of Meredith Emerson. The citation issued to Gary Hilton from the National Forest in Florida was also stained with her blood.

The Transylvania County authorities briefed the group on their investigation of the murder of Irene Bryant and the disappearance of John Bryant in October. The Ducktown investigator provided a photograph of the person who had accessed the Bryants' bank account. There was no doubt that the image captured by the ATM camera was Gary Hilton.

The FBI Behavioral Science Unit arrived shortly after 11:00 and expressed their interest in Hilton's activities. Now, Gary Hilton by the FBI's definition is a serial killer. To fit that definition, someone has to have killed three or more people, with a cooling-off period in between each one.

At noon, the group traveled to a local Catholic church that had agreed to let us use their community hall for a working lunch. Everyone shared more information, and together we formed strategies. In the back of my mind, I couldn't help but think about the status of Hilton's cooperation. I wanted to know where Meredith was.

The tip line continued to receive calls reporting sightings of Hilton in Dawson Forest the previous week. One caller reported that on Friday, January 4, at 10:15 a.m., his GPS had directed him to Shoal Creek Road by mistake. While driving, his truck became stuck just off the road. He then saw a white male and a dog standing next to a white van, which was parked about three hundred yards away in the woods. It was the same man he had seen in a photograph of on the news. He mentioned to the man that he was going to call the police in order to get a wrecker to help pull his truck from the ditch. The man tried to talk him out of calling the police, and after learning the call had already been made, immediately loaded his van with items at the campsite and left.

Bobby McElwee continued to lead search teams in Dawson Forest, and additional helicopter support had been requested. There was a lot of activity that morning on the hunch that there we would find Meredith Emerson.

After lunch, we returned to my office and continued our discussions. We were able to talk by phone with the Florida Department of Law Enforcement (FDLE) and investigators with the Leon County Sheriff's Office in Tallahassee about the murder of Cheryl Dunlap in December. They were making plans to come meet with us and share the evidence they had gathered down there. At about two o'clock, my cell phone displayed the number for the prosecutor in Union County. I stepped out of the meeting and listened as he told me Hilton was ready to tell me where Meredith was. The prosecutor had formally agreed to take the death penalty off the table and had discussed with Meredith's parents over the weekend to make sure they supported that decision. I informed the group of this development, and even though this was what we had hoped would happen, everyone seemed to pause as if they were thinking about poor Meredith.

Before I left the office, I thought about Meredith's parents and the telephone call they would get from me later that night. I thought about her roommate, Julia, and all Meredith's friends who would hear the news reports that would surely come once the word got out that we had her. I had to stay focused and make sure nothing happened to cause Hilton to change his mind.

The drive through the winding mountain road across Blood Mountain to the Union County jail took almost an hour. The GBI director was with me, and we were followed by Clay Bridges. When we arrived, I spoke with the prosecutor and Hilton's lawyer to discuss the ground rules for the interview. We expected Hilton to be cooperative and noncombative. Present in the room would be Hilton and his lawyer, Clay, and myself. At 4:55 p.m., Clay activated his digital recorder and we began the interview.

*Cagle: If you'll tell me the area.*

*Hilton: Yeah, I'm going to show you right here.*

*Cagle: Okay. All right.*

*Hilton: It's Dawson Forest.*

*Cagle: Dawson Forest. Okay, I'm familiar with that area.*

*Hilton: Oh, good. It's a nice place, isn't it? It's the City of Atlanta Tract.*

*Cagle: Okay.*

*Hilton: Make a right on Dawson Forest Road. Go to Shoal Creek Road, which becomes dirt. There is [sic] several gated roads off to the west side. They're gated and the gates are closed, and they are designed as trails. They are heavily used equestrian trails. I believe it is the first road to the left.*

*Cagle: Okay.*

*Hilton: To make sure you're on the right road, immediately to the north of that road, on either side of Shoal Creek, is a sign that says no bicycles beyond this point.*

*Cagle: How far down the road?*

*Hilton: Go down the road about fifty yards, and it's going to be off the south side or the left side of the road. The body will be.*

*Cagle: Okay.*

*Hilton: A landmark for that would be the trail is double-blazed where two trails come together. One is lavender and the other is gray.*

*Cagle: Okay.*

*Hilton: Okay, the body will be approximately forty yards, or 120 feet. It's covered by leaves and brush.*

*Cagle: You said the body is down there on the left of the road under some leaves and brush.*

*Hilton: Under just a pile of leaves and brush, but not buried.*

*Cagle: Okay, is it wrapped in anything?*

*Hilton: No, it isn't.*

*Cagle: Is it clothed?*

*Hilton: No, it isn't.*

*Cagle: Is it intact?*

*Hilton: No, it isn't.*

*Cagle: You want to talk some more about that?*

*Hilton: Okay, the head will be missing.*

*Cagle: Where's the head?*

*Hilton: The only reason, by the way, the head was removed was forensically.*

*Cagle: Yeah, right.*

*Hilton: In other words, in the hair are fibers. And that's the only reason.*

*Cagle: Where will the head be?*

*Hilton: To locate that, continue north on Shoal Creek Road, and I believe it will be about the second gated road, approximately a half a mile on the left. The road is on a ridge line, and it's got a gate across it. You're going to need a dog for this, I believe.*

*Cagle: Can you help us?*

*Hilton: I'll help. It's uncomfortable for me to go there, though. If I've got to help you, I'm going to help you.*

*Cagle: We are going to take you down there.*

*Hilton: There's a bunch of trees cut down edging the road. These are tree trunks about forty yards down the road.*

*Bridges: Is that the only portion of the body that's missing?*

*Hilton: That is all. And I should mention there's cloth-ing there too. If you put a dog on it, you will come up with it like that. I apologize to both of you guys. It's been trying for you. I'm sure these cases are emotionally wrenching. But that's your damn job (laughs).*

As I walked out of the interview room, memories of that spooky place returned vividly. The old nuclear site. I knew exactly where Hilton was talking about—I had been there in 1972.

I briefed the prosecutor and GBI director as we prepared Hilton for the ride to Dawson Forest. Clay Bridges would be with Hilton and his lawyer in the jail transport van, and I would go ahead of them. The director would take Clay's car back to my office and then come to the forest.

Dawsonville is the county seat for Dawson County, about an hour and a half from the Union County jail. I called Agent Bobby McElwee to let him know there would be at least two crime scenes in Dawson Forest and that we were bringing Hilton with us in case we needed him to show us where they were. I also called our crime-scene units and instructed them to be on their way to meet Bobby. One last phone call was made to Kevin Tanner, a close friend of mine who was the chief deputy of the Dawson County Sheriff's Office. I let him know the latest information and con-firmed he had investigators available to help.

I arrived at the forest at about 6:45. It had been dark almost an hour, and although it wasn't as cold as it had been, it was still uncomfortable. Bobby and his search team were waiting at the gate on Shoal Creek Road that Hilton had described. I gave them the directions that would lead them down the road to a point where they would then turn left into the woods. After only fifteen minutes, I received a radio call from Bobby saying he found her. DNR Ranger William Thacker arrived and opened the gate, allowing the crime-scene units to get closer to the scene.

Their flashlights cut deep into the woods. Walking through these woods in the daytime is a challenge, but at night it becomes much more difficult. After leaving the thick brush, the forest leveled a bit and I could see an area cordoned off with crime-scene tape. An area about six feet long had been marked with red flags. Small tree branches were being removed from atop a mound that appeared to be three to four feet tall. Photographs of the scene had been taken, and soon the body of Meredith Emerson was exposed. Her nude, decapitated body shocked all of us. The smell of bleach lingered all around. A small oak tree about six inches in diameter was coated with bloodstains about four feet from the ground. A bloodstained serrated kitchen knife was also found at the scene, with the blade broken.

At about 7:30, the jail transport van containing Gary Hilton arrived at Dawson Forest. The person most familiar with the forest would certainly be Ranger William Thacker. So, following Hilton's directions to the second scene, he and I drove about a half mile north on Shoal Creek Road followed by the transport van. We arrived at a small road leading to a locked gate just north of Shoal Creek. I was not confident that we could find the scene without Hilton's help. The clatter of leg chains was prominent as we walked him up the small road, and after about fifty yards, we stopped. Hilton and his guards remained in the roadway as William and I entered the woods to the right. Up over the bank and about thirty yards in, a large tree trunk lay on the ground. We walked to the left end of the tree, and there we found tennis shoes and a bloody fleece. We walked toward the other end, where I pushed back leaves and debris. I came upon a mound of leaves that was higher than others and carefully moved the leaves and sticks away. And there she was.

William and I sat there without saying a word. I silently told Meredith we would do everything we could to see that Hilton would never do this to anyone again. I asked William to stay with her while I went back to make sure Hilton was taken back to the jail and to arrange for another crime-scene unit to come. There has never been a time I wanted to kill someone as badly as I wanted to kill Gary Hilton that night. I just told his guards to get him out of there. William remained in the woods with Meredith until he was replaced by other crime-scene specialists.

Shoal Creek Road has spotty cell phone service, so I drove out of the forest to get a better signal. I had to call Meredith's parents to let them know we had found her before they heard about it on the news. There were no reporters in the forest, but there were enough searchers for me to know that word would leak out. Her parents were staying with Doug and Peggy Bailey in Athens, and as I dialed Peggy's number, I tried to compose myself. When Peggy answered, I told her we had found Meredith and asked her to tell the Emersons. I could hear the deep sadness in her voice as she told me she would. I let her know we were still working the crime scene in Dawson Forest and that it would take a while. I made no mention of the decapitation. After the call, I sat there and realized I needed to fulfill my obligation to tell them everything, so I called back. Again Peggy answered, and this time I told her everything. Over the past several days, Peggy had acted as the family spokesperson and was present at all my briefings with Meredith's parents. She was supportive of them and the investigation. And now she was going to give them this news.

Before I returned to the forest and out of cell phone range, John Bankhead, the GBI public information officer, called and said there would be a news conference in about an hour at a nearby elementary school to release the information about the recovery of Meredith.

The satellite news trucks were arriving at the school and the reporters were gathering in an area inside that had been prepared for the news conference. Many of the same reporters were there who had been at Vogel State Park the week before. I think the plan was to go live for the eleven o'clock news shows. I came into the school from the back door into a classroom to prepare the information to be released. I knew they would ask where the information came from that had led us to Meredith's body. I was willing to disclose that Hilton had provided that information, but I was not willing to talk about any deals he had made with the Union County prosecutor. Discussion of those decisions must only be released by the prosecutors. Now, of course, we were in a different jurisdiction, and the Dawson County prosecutor would take the lead. I was also not willing to talk about or disclose that she had been decapitated.

I had known the Dawson County prosecutor for over twenty years and considered him a friend. He arrived at the school with one of his investigators and two of his assistants and came straight to me demanding to know why he had not been informed that we were searching for Meredith Emerson in "his county." After spending the last week managing this investigation and the last few hours in both crime scenes in the forest, I was in no mood to listen to foolish questions. I responded in a way that caused me to remember I only had a couple of months to retire. I thought I could certainly hold on for that time and retire before they could fire me. The director was within earshot of my response to the prosecutor, but he never said a word. I guess I was safe for the time being. The prosecutor turned and walked away, but came back in a few minutes to apologize.

I bet there were at least ten people behind me as we entered the room for the press conference. Some of them had not even been involved in the investigation, but I suppose they wanted to be seen on TV. They lined up behind me in front of the cameras, and I began my prepared remarks releasing the fact that we had recovered Meredith in the Dawson Forest Wildlife Management Area a few miles away. I told them Gary Hilton had disclosed earlier in the afternoon where she was. The first question, as I had anticipated, was what deal had been made with Hilton. I had the answer to that question already written on my notepad: "I'm not prepared to talk about any agreements made with Gary Hilton." I also had anticipated questions about the time it would take to work the crime scene: "If we are not able to complete the crime-scene process in the night, we will secure the scene and finish at daybreak."

One reporter in the back, whom I'd not seen at Vogel, repeated the question and got the same answer. He asked the same question again, but in a different way, and as before, I was in no mood to answer foolish questions. I said, "We will be through with the crime scene when we are through with the crime scene." I would later learn that a large group of officers in South Georgia who were watching the news thought that was a great answer. I guess it was obvious, though, to the GBI director that I was about to lose it on national television, so he stepped forward and began to take questions. The same reporter would later complain that I had been "too gruff" with him. But again, only two more months to retire. The news conference ended and I returned to the forest.

There were two priorities at the scenes that needed to be completed soon: we had to recover the body of Meredith and her head before we could leave that night. The rest could be done in the morning. By midnight, the coroner had taken custody of her remains, later to be transported to the crime lab. The scene was going to be secured by deputies until we could return at daybreak to finish. I got to my cabin at about two a.m., where I poured myself a stiff drink.

And then I remembered. Railroad tracks. That summer job in '72, and the railcars loaded with items to be irradiated. The railroad tracks, long since removed, would have been near Meredith.

A couple of nights ago, when I left the Huddle House where Hilton had earlier made a phone call, I had only been a few miles from Meredith, who was alive. Why hadn't I thought about Dawson Forest?

# 11

*It's so fucking dreadful that all you can do is do your duty and go on autopilot. But why I chose to kill was sociopathic rage against society.*

—Gary Michael Hilton

The crime-scene specialists worked through the morning to finish processing the scenes in Dawson Forest. Gary Hilton was transported from the Union County jail to the Dawson County Adult Detention Center, and Clay Bridges obtained an arrest warrant charging him with murder in Dawson County. The kidnapping charge in Union would eventually be dismissed.

Members of the media gathered outside the detention center in hopes of seeing Hilton arrive. He was brought in through a secure area not in view of the public. At about noon, the autopsy on the body of Meredith Emerson was completed. A short news conference took place there in the parking lot, and I announced the results to the reporters I had gotten to know at Vogel:

> "Meredith Emerson died of blunt-force trauma to the head. Following her death, she was decapitated."

The looks on their faces revealed the sadness in their hearts. No questions were asked. They looked exhausted, like everyone else. They quietly packed up their gear and returned to their studios in Atlanta.

As the days continued in January, calls poured into my office with inquiries from several law enforcement agencies around the

United States about missing hikers in their jurisdictions. Gary Hilton's travels were important for them to know.

On December 7, 2005, Rosanna Miliani, twenty-six, walked into a store in Bryson City, North Carolina, with an older man. According to the clerk, the man said he was a preacher who would preach at campsites on the nearby Appalachian Trail. The clerk remembered that Rosanna seemed nervous. The man bought a hiking bag. That was the last time Rosanna was seen alive. Two years later, after seeing photographs of Gary Hilton in our case, the store clerk called the authorities in North Carolina reporting that he believed the person he had seen with Rosanna was Hilton.

Two years later, on December 6, 2007, the torso and legs of Michael Scot Louis, twenty-seven, were discovered in plastic trash bags inside Tomoka State Park in South Daytona Beach, Florida. His head was never found. No definitive connection could be made to Hilton in either case, but the method of operation (MO) was similar.

A memorial service was scheduled for Meredith in Athens, Georgia, on January 11. Other family and friends came from Colorado and joined hundreds at the church that morning. When I arrived in the parking lot, members of the news media whom I had gotten to know were also there. Volunteers who did not even know Meredith but had helped search for her on Blood Mountain came by the dozens. I was a little apprehensive, as I did not know how I would be received. After all, we hadn't saved Meredith. There are some who will say the police didn't do enough, you know.

Meredith's brother and parents and other family members came into the church from the side door and were kept in a private room until the service. I walked into the sanctuary and sat in a pew near the front. Some were not able find seats and stood in the back. The service lasted for about an hour, and it was a sad time.

I don't think there was a dry eye, including my own. Following the service, food was provided in a large community room in the basement of the church. There, I said goodbye to the Emersons. They were leaving for Colorado with Ella the next day. I would later attend another memorial service for Meredith in Colorado.

Agents from the Florida Department of Law Enforcement and deputies from the Leon County Sheriff's Office came to the office later in the week to learn more about the evidence we had that they might use in their case in Florida. After learning that Cheryl Dunlap's rear tire looked as though it had been purposely punctured, we informed them that we had recovered a military-style knife just off the trail on Blood Mountain. We relinquished the knife to them so it could be compared with the tire at their crime lab. We also told them we had recovered several things that were bloodstained, but our crime lab would probably not test all of them. That would have to be done at their lab. We would provide them with all of the evidence when our case was over.

As the month continued, the paperwork came together and negotiations with Gary Hilton and his lawyers began. The deal to take the death penalty off the table had been made by one prosecutor, but now this prosecutor was considering reneging. This would serve no purpose, I thought. We were convinced that Hilton would be prosecuted in Florida and North Carolina later, and the death penalty, I was sure, would be sought somewhere. After all, Florida seems to have an express lane to the death chamber, as their cases travel quickly through the appeals process.

A deal was eventually reached, and on January 31, 2008, at 9:00 a.m., Gary Hilton was indicted in Dawson County Superior Court for the murder of Meredith Emerson. Her parents and Doug and Peggy Bailey arrived at the courthouse just after noon. Hilton was scheduled to plead guilty at one o'clock. I stayed with them in a room just off the courtroom. A knock on the door signaled it was time for them to enter the courtroom, and I led them to their seats just behind the prosecution table. Security was tight that day and the courtroom quickly filled up. Hilton was brought in wearing a red jumpsuit, leg chains, handcuffs, and a bulletproof vest, and sat with his lawyers at the defense table. Bonnie Oliver, the judge, entered the courtroom and got down to business. She asked Hilton the required questions, and after hearing him say he desired to plead guilty, she accepted his plea. Susan and Dave Emerson requested to make a statement, and as they spoke, sobbing was heard throughout the room.

Susan read her statement:

> "I'm not sorry that the death penalty was taken off the table. That would have been an easy out. Let him stay alive and slowly rot. God may choose to forgive him; however, he is not worth the time and energy it would take me to do so. My focus will remain on all the good Meredith stood for and still does."

Dave Emerson read his statement:

> "My daughter was a shining light in our lives, and now we are left with a hole in our hearts that will not heal. I feel no punishment is too severe for Mr. Hilton. Only pray that he suffers immensely for his heinous acts and that his fellow inmates recognize his evil and malevolence for mankind and treat him with appropriate measures."

Hilton was asked if he wished to make a statement. He said no.

Judge Oliver sentenced Gary Hilton to life in prison and made the following statement:

> "Let there be no mistake, the court is not intending mercy on you due to your age, but rather recognizes in the natural course of things you likely will die

of natural causes before any sentence of death the state might obtain could be carried out."

Hilton was quickly taken from the courtroom and moved next door to the jail. Meredith's parents and Doug and Peggy were taken back to the room as before to wait a while as the spectators left the courtroom. They seemed satisfied with the sentence. However, I knew there would be some, those who didn't have any direct knowledge of the investigation, who would criticize the decision to not seek the death penalty. I was right. After the courthouse cleared out, we took the Emersons and Baileys down the stairs to an awaiting car, and they left without the media knowing. With that, our case was over, and we now turned our attention to Florida and North Carolina.

As part of the North Carolina investigation, the FBI in Asheville obtained buccal swabs from Marc and Robert Bryant, the children of John and Irene, and sent them to our crime lab to compare with the unidentified bloodstain discovered on the driver's seat in Gary Hilton's van. The results read:

> The donor of the primary profile from the section of driver's seat is an individual who is not excluded as the biological father of Robert Bryant and Marc Bryant.

On February 5, human skeletal remains found by a hunter in Macon County, North Carolina, about seventy-five feet from a locked forest service road in the Nantahala National Forest, were identified as those of John Bryant. A bone fragment was sent to our DNA section, and on February 27, the lab issued the following:

> With a reasonable scientific certainty it can be concluded that the DNA obtained from the section of driver seat matches John Bryant or his identical sibling.

Also in February, the FDLE lab was able to determine that a knife we found on Blood Mountain had caused the puncture in Cheryl Dunlap's tire. On February 28, Gary Hilton was indicted in Leon County, Florida, for the murder of Cheryl Dunlap.

It was clear to me that we had made the right decision by taking the death penalty off the table in exchange for the body of Meredith Emerson. It was also clear that, based on the evidence we recovered, there was a real probability that North Carolina or Florida would kill Gary Hilton.

# 12

*Supermax. Eric Rudolph went there, and he only killed two people. And he's at supermax. So it's where they send the notorious, infamous people. Okay, they're sending my ass to supermax.*

—Gary Michael Hilton

For the first few weeks of February, we continued to receive information about Gary Hilton and those who had encountered him. The way he confronted people and sometimes threatened them in the forest seemed to be a consistent behavior. Agents were putting together a timeline of his travels over the last several years. No definitive information was developed indicating that his travels corresponded with missing hikers in states other than North Carolina, Florida, and Georgia.

In late February, a rift began to form between the United States Attorney's Office in Asheville and the State Attorney's Office in Tallahassee. We had the mother lode of evidence that certainly would help convict Hilton in both locations. However, the US attorney wanted all the evidence relinquished to the FBI crime lab in Quantico, Virginia, and the State's attorney wanted the evidence given to the FDLE lab (it's common for prosecutors to want their own lab scientists to perform tests, as they have better control). I was stuck in the middle. Before things really got out of hand, I invited everyone to Atlanta to work it out. After two hours of heated discussions and calls back and forth to the prospective labs, we agreed that Florida would get the evidence. The Florida crime lab then agreed to send their scientist to North Carolina to testify at their trial. They also agreed to analyze and test all blood evidence found. These two factors seemed to calm everyone down. Or at least, they made the final decision easier. By the middle of March, we relinquished all evidence to them.

On February 28, 2008, Gary Hilton was indicted in Tallahassee, Florida, for the murder of Cheryl Dunlap. The Florida lab had discovered blood on the shoelace of a boot we recovered in our case and matched it to a DNA profile developed from Dunlap's toothbrush.

As March rolled around, my time was short. Only one month left until I retired. The GBI director arranged for the bureau psychologist to come to my office and meet with all the agents. Even though this investigation had been relatively short compared to others, I think he could tell it had affected us all. The psychologist identified symptoms of post-traumatic stress disorder (PTSD): inability to sleep, difficulty concentrating, and excessive drinking, among others. I think we all qualified.

On Friday, March 28, the contents of my desk and office were boxed up ready for me to move. A couple of agents helped me take them to my personal truck, as I had already turned in my bureau car. I was having trouble believing it was actually going to be over. The hope I had of ending my career without any more major cases had been dashed. Instead, I was going to end it with perhaps the most important case I've ever worked. Meredith Emerson was the child most parents would dream of having. Gary Hilton was the nightmare most parents would like to forget. Leaving the job was going to be tough, but leaving this case would be impossible.

On April 1, I officially retired from the GBI. But I never truly retired from this case.

# 13

## THE MEREDITH EMERSON MEMORIAL PRIVACY ACT

*As for the disposition of crime-scene photos,*
*it's the publisher's decision what to publish, not mine.*

—Fred Rosen

It had been two years since I left the GBI and I was trying to move on, as most do in retirement. I kept up with the cases in Florida and North Carolina, but my time as a decision maker was long gone. Florida was getting close to a trial date, I heard, and North Carolina was waiting to see what happened down there. I missed a lot of the action and hoped my former agents would keep me in the loop. But these things take time, especially since Florida was seeking the death penalty.

In January 2010, my cell phone rang and the caller ID displayed the name Mark Jackson, GBI's director of legal services. Mark and I had worked drug cases together many years ago. While working as an agent, he went to law school at night and now represented the bureau. He told me he had received an open records request in the Meredith Emerson case specifically requesting copies of the crime-scene photographs. He was concerned; at that time, Georgia had no law preventing the disclosure of crime-scene pictures. The disturbing part was that the request had been made by a reporter representing *Hustler* magazine.

Fred Rosen, who claimed to be a successful author of several true crime books, was behind the request. I later asked him if he was such a successful author, why associate himself with a rag porn magazine like *Hustler*? He said he had to make a living. So much for the successful author story!

My response to Mark Jackson was quick: "Don't do it." Georgia had laws preventing the distribution of autopsy photographs, and in this case, there was little difference. We had to do something to keep from disclosing these pictures.

A friend of mine was the first person I thought to call. David Ralston was actually the Speaker of the Georgia House of Representatives and a powerful legislator. I left him an urgent message asking that he call me. He did very quickly, and I explained the situation to him. The legislature was in session, and he told me to meet him at the capital the next morning. The next day, David began to fast-track a new law. In the meantime, legal action to stop the disclosure was taken on behalf of the Emerson family by an attorney close to Meredith's friends. A judge quickly barred the bureau from complying with *Hustler*'s records request. Over the next few weeks, draft legislation was written to prevent future dissemination of graphic images of genitalia, dismemberment, or decapitation of a crime victim.

On March 29, 2010, the Meredith Emerson Memorial Privacy Act was signed into law, preventing disclosure of certain types of crime-scene photographs without the direction of a judge.

# 14

## JUSTICE FOR CHERYL DUNLAP

*If they want to spend a million, and then another million to get death, and then another eight million to defend the death penalty, hey they can do that.*

—Gary Michael Hilton

On January 31, 2011, three years after Gary Hilton was sentenced to life in prison in Georgia for the murder of Meredith Emerson, the Tallahassee trial began. The pre-trial motions in death-penalty cases sometimes take years to be argued and ruled on by judges, but now everything was ready. Death-penalty trials have two phases: the guilt/innocence portion, and if there is a conviction, the second part, called the penalty phase, begins. The same jury makes both decisions. The rules of evidence prevented the Florida State attorney from presenting evidence from our case in the guilt/innocence portion of the trial.

Jury selection began with over two hundred potential jurors summoned. State attorney Willie Meggs gave an overview of the case informing the jurors of Cheryl Dunlap's disappearance on December 1, 2007. The judge told the potential jurors that if selected, the trial could last a couple of weeks, and there was a possibility they would be sequestered, meaning kept together overnight. One potential juror recalled being in the North Georgia mountains in 2007 during the time we were investigating the disappearance of Meredith Emerson and seeing Hilton at a camp store. He was excused. Questioning continued for two days, and the number of prospective jurors went down to eighty. These jurors were questioned about their opinions of capital punishment. A few said they could not impose the death penalty. The rest were asked if they could find Gary Hilton guilty knowing the death penalty was a possibility. They all said they could. The prosecutors read a list of potential witnesses, forty of whom would be law enforcement officers. Other expert witnesses would testify as well.

On February 2, at about nine p.m., six men and six women were selected to hear the evidence against Gary Hilton. Two alternate jurors were designated in case any of the main ones were unable to finish the trial.

On February 4, Hilton's lawyer made a request to delay the trial, telling the judge she had not had enough time to prepare. Her request was denied, and testimony began.

Michael Shirley testified that he and his wife saw Cheryl Dunlap alone on a trail in the Apalachicola National Forest December 1, 2007. She was reading a red book. A few days later, after seeing Dunlap's picture in the paper, he and his wife went back to where they had seen her. On their way out of the forest, they saw the red book on the side of the road. He directed deputy sheriffs to the book.

Terrese Johnson testified she was at a gas station in Bristol, Florida, when a man came up to her stating she looked like the lady who had been murdered. She later identified the man as Gary Hilton.

Testimony continued, and at approximately 9:30 p.m., Ronnie Rentz testified that on December 15, while hunting in the National Forest, he saw buzzards circling an object. Upon inspection, it appeared to be a torso, legs, and feet. He called the police, who arrived and determined the body was missing its head and hands.

On February 7, Ronald Weyland, a deputy with the Orange County Sheriff's Office, testified that he had enhanced video surveillance taken at an ATM in Tallahassee on December 2, 3, and 4. The man depicted in the photographs had worn a blue dress shirt all three days and appeared to have used a mask and some type of athletic tape to cover his face. In Florida, jurors are allowed to ask questions, and one asked Weyland if he could estimate the man's height. He said he could not.

FDLE Crime Lab Analyst Amy George testified that when Dunlap's body had been found, she responded to the scene. She testified that the body was covered with limbs and palmetto frays. George had also examined a fire pit at a campsite in the forest, where she found hand and skull bones. A bead was also found in the pit. Similar beads were later located in Dunlap's car.

Associate Medical Examiner Dr. Anthony Clark had performed the autopsy on the body found in the forest. The autopsy photographs were admitted into evidence and showed that the body was missing its head and hands. He testified that he had listed the cause of death as "undetermined homicidal violence."

Mitchell Posey, one of my agents, testified about the evidence collected in the QuikTrip dumpster on January 4, 2008. A trash bag full of evidence had been collected, along with a Florida forest service citation issued to Gary Hilton on December 28. The judge admitted into evidence some of these items, to include three metal chains, padlocks, and a collapsible nightstick. A pair of nylon pants and a pair of hiking boots were also admitted.

On February 9, Dr. Anthony Falsetti, a forensic anthropologist, testified that he had examined the bones recovered from the fire pit in the national forest and determined them to be human. He said the hands were those of an adult man or woman with small hands. He chose bones with the least amount of burning to analyze for DNA. The FDLE crime lab sent him vertebrae in order to look for trauma, and he determined there were seven cut marks, indicating a sharp-force injury.

Patricia Aagaard, a forensic mitochondrial DNA examiner for the FBI, testified as an expert DNA examiner. She explained to the jury that mitochondrial DNA is inherited maternally, while nuclear DNA is specific to one person. She tested the bones for mitochondrial DNA, but they were too badly burned to produce reliable results.

On February 10, Lieutenant Mark Cecci with the Union County Sheriff's Office testified about finding a bayonet on the Blood Mountain approach trail in January 2008.

Tool mark expert Jeff Foggy, with the Florida Department of Law Enforcement, testified that he had made comparisons and tested sections of Cheryl Dunlap's punctured tire. Each knife, he said, leaves its own unique pattern. After receiving the bayonet recovered on Blood Mountain, he concluded that it had made the cut in Dunlap's tire.

On February 11, jurors listened to a recording of Gary Hilton's interaction with the Leon County deputies who transported him from Georgia to Tallahassee in June 2008:

> "I'm not all bad, as I'm sure you can see. I'm a fuck-ing genius, as you can see. There are two kinds of bayonet fighters, good ones and dead ones."

Amy George, an FDLE crime-lab analyst, testified about locating twenty-five swabs of suspected blood she had collected from inside Hilton's van.

JoEllen Brown, another FDLE crime-lab analyst, testified that she examined body fluids and was an expert in DNA analysis and population statistics. She had been able to match DNA obtained from Cheryl Dunlap's toothbrush to the body recovered from the woods. She screened 750 items for blood in an effort to extract DNA. Brown also tested the boots from the dumpster in Georgia and found additional blood. The shoestring gave results of three people, the majority belonging to Cheryl Dunlap. Brown was given swabs from Dunlap's thighs and found DNA that had degraded, but was still a possible match to Gary Hilton.

She detected blood on several items of evidence that had been taken from Hilton's van when he was arrested in Georgia. She tested a blue sleeping bag and found blood in nine areas. The blood contained Hilton's DNA, with the other major contributor identified as Cheryl Dunlap. The DNA, she testified, could only belong to one individual in eleven trillion, and because there are not one trillion people on the planet, it would be unlikely that the DNA was not Dunlap's.

Caleb Wynn, the Leon County correctional officer, testified he had overheard Hilton talking to a fellow inmate at the jail:

> "He said the only thing he regretted is getting caught. If he had a second chance, he'd do it right."

On June 6, 2008, three officers had driven Hilton from Georgia to Florida. Hilton spoke nonstop, and his statements were recorded. The State played portions of this recording:

> "I'm not all bad. I mean, you got to understand, I mean, I'm sure you can see. I mean, I'm a fucking genius, man. I'm not a—I'm not all bad. I just, you know, lost my mind for a little bit. Lost my grip on myself, man. What can I tell you? FBI and everybody else is trying to scratch their head; guys don't get started doing my shit at sixty-one years old. It just don't happen, you know. Like there's a retired FBI named Clifford Van Zandt that keeps getting himself in the news, talking about me. And he said, this guy didn't just fall off the turnip truck, he said. You know, in other words, he's been doing this. But like I told you before, you know, when I saw you before, I said, remember, I said I'd give you one for free. Nothing before September, okay? I mean, I'm not joking, okay? I just, I got old and sick and couldn't make a living and just lost, flat lost my booking mind for a while, man. I couldn't grip on."

Following this testimony, the prosecution rested their case.

Gary Hilton's defense lawyers did not have much to work with. The State's case was overwhelming. After calling a few witnesses to dispute some of the State's experts, they rested their case as well.

The jury deliberated for about one hour and found Gary Hilton guilty of the murder of Cheryl Dunlap.

Anticipating the guilty verdict, Clay Bridges and I were on our way to Tallahassee. Clay would be called as a witness in the penalty phase to testify to all the circumstances of our investigation. I wanted to watch his testimony.

The penalty phase of the trial, using the same jury that had convicted Gary Hilton in the first phase, began. Clay was called to testify about the abduction and murder of Meredith Emerson. Family and friends of Cheryl Dunlap testified about her good character and how much she would be missed. There was no doubt this was the tipping point for the jury. Hilton's defense team attempted to suggest that he had committed these murders because of a traumatic head injury received as a child when a Murphy bed had fallen on him. The jury did not buy it and returned a recommendation to the judge that Gary Hilton be put to death. The judge followed the recommendation.

While I was in the courthouse, a guy approached me saying he was a producer for NBC working on a story for their *Dateline* series. He asked me if I would participate. I told him I would not unless NBC agreed to certain conditions: that they be respectful to the memory of Meredith Emerson, that they not sensationalize the manner in which she died, that they make no attempt to interview her parents, and that they tell the truth. They agreed, and on August 11, 2011, a two-hour *Dateline* episode called "The Mystery on Blood Mountain" aired providing the details regarding the death of John and Irene Bryant in North Carolina, Cheryl Dunlap in Florida, and Meredith Emerson in Georgia.

Over the years, I had stayed in touch with Meredith's parents in Colorado. They were trying their best to move on. After seeing or hearing about *Dateline*, they sent me an email expressing their disappointment in me for participating. They requested I not contact them again. I was devastated, but complied.

# 15

## JUSTICE FOR JOHN
## AND IRENE BRYANT

*They found a skull and a pelvis, and it's off of Old Murphy Road, and it's on a Forest Service Rd., and they found the body, so maybe. . . . He's no longer missing.*

—Gary Michael Hilton

In June 2011, a federal grand jury in the Western District of North Carolina indicted Gary Hilton for kidnapping, robbery, and the murder of John Bryant in the Nantahala National Forest. Hilton also admitted to killing Irene Bryant in the Pisgah National Forest. On March 27, 2012, just a month before his trial date, Gary Hilton pleaded guilty. During the hearing and before the judge could accept the plea, the government had to provide a factual basis that Hilton would ultimately be found guilty by a jury if the case were to go to trial. The assistant US attorney provided the following to the judge:

> During the month of October 2007, Hilton was living in his Chevrolet Astro van in the Pisgah Natural Forest. On October 21, 2007, John and Irene Bryant encountered Hilton while hiking in the forest. Irene was attacked and killed. Her body was later discovered near where they parked their car. John was kidnapped by Hilton and was forced to provide his bank ATM PIN number. Hilton then took John in his van to the Nantahala National Forest and shot him in the head with a .22 magnum firearm.
>
> On October 22, 2007, at about 7:37 p.m., Hilton used the Bryant's ATM card in Ducktown, Tenn., to withdraw $300. Photos from the bank's security

cameras show a slender person wearing a yellow raincoat covering his face.

Hilton's attorneys did not object to the facts as stated by the government. The judge asked Hilton if he was in fact guilty. Hilton said yes, and the judge accepted his guilty plea.

In the federal court system, judges are required to order a pre-sentence investigation before sentencing. Federal probation officers collected background information about Hilton, including his upbringing, educational background, military service, and employment history. Any prior criminal convictions would also be relevant. By now, Hilton had been convicted in Georgia for killing Meredith Emerson and was awaiting execution in Florida after being convicted for the murder of Cheryl Dunlap. Since the death penalty was not being sought, the only sentencing option was life without parole in federal prison.

On April 26, 2013, I drove to the federal courthouse in Asheville for the sentencing. I hoped the end of this last case would provide some closure for the Bryant family. And for the Dunlap and Emerson families. And for me. The last few years, it seemed, I had struggled more and more with this case. *We did all we could,* I kept telling myself, *and we caught the guy, thus preventing him from killing again.* But it didn't feel like enough. When I had been at the Huddle House after Hilton called his former employer, I was so close to his campsite. And Meredith had been alive. Why had I not thought of Dawson Forest?

I took a seat behind the prosecution table in the huge, old courtroom. Holly Bryant, the daughter of John and Irene, and Bob, their son, sat behind me. Hilton was led into the courtroom in chains and sat with his lawyer at the defense table. US District Judge Martin Reidinger entered the courtroom and took his seat at the bench. The courtroom clerk announced the case: "The United States of America vs. Gary Michael Hilton, for sentencing." It is standard for both sides to receive the presentence report prior to Hilton being sentenced, and the judge inquired if they had. Both sides acknowledged they had received the report. The judge asked if there were any objections to it as written. Neither side objected to the contents of the report. This was simply a formality, since everyone knew what the final sentence would be. The judge adopted the findings and recommendations of the report as submitted. He asked if anyone wished to speak. Gary Hilton, for the first time, made a statement:

"Your Honor, I do have remorse. I am sorry."

Holly Bryant slowly stood and addressed the judge:

"He will spend the rest of his life and die in a cage, or at the hands of a Florida executioner. But the main thing, he will never get out to harm anyone again. For him to laughingly say he's sorry is a slap in the face. He beat my mother in the head. He shot my father in the head. Sorry is not enough."

Bob Bryant addressed the judge as well:

"I wanted a bullet in his head, and I think they should have done it five years ago."

Judge Reidinger sentenced Hilton to four consecutive life sentences without the possibility for parole. As the marshals led him out of the courtroom, he turned to me and winked. Looks like he remembered me from our interview and trip to the forest the night we recovered Meredith. So much for remorse. A few days later, he was on his way back to Florida's death row.

Hilton appealed his conviction in Florida on several grounds, including when the trial court had erred by admitting certain evidence at his trial. Specifically, portions of the tape recording of his statements made while he was being transported from Georgia to Florida in 2008. The Florida Supreme Court did not agree and denied the appeal on March 31, 2013. As is usually the case, the next appeal to be filed alleged that he had failed to receive effective assistance of counsel during his original trial. The appeals court disagreed, and his second appeal was denied in November 2018. This was his final state appeal. Federal appeals would be next.

The drive back to my cabin that night took about four hours. The sentence in North Carolina was not unexpected, since it had been negotiated and agreed to by both sides, and had prevented the case from dragging on for many more years. If only Florida could just get on with it and kill Gary Hilton. But that day would be worth the wait.

# 16

## REMEMBERING MEREDITH

*At the time, there were a lot of 5Ks and runs in the community. How can we do something different and honor Meredith?*

—Julia Karrenbauer

After I retired from the GBI, I worked at the sheriff's office in Dawson County for almost six years. It was a good department, and the crime rate was low compared to that of other counties nearby. It was rare to have violent crime, much less a murder, but if one occurred, it was usually easy to figure out who committed it. It was hard to believe it had been five years since we had recovered the body of Meredith Emerson. Time had moved on, but those days would be forever fixed in the minds of many. A few of the agents who had worked on that case back then were retired now. Clay Bridges had been assigned to a drug unit, but still worked and lived in North Georgia. DNR Ranger William Thacker had retired not long after I did in 2008, and was still the expert on Dawson Forest.

Following the death of Meredith in 2008, her former roommate, Julia, and other friends formed a non-profit called Right to Hike. They helped support a scholarship fund in Meredith's name allowing students at the University of Georgia to travel abroad in France, as Meredith once had. They also held fundraisers to raise money to support hiking safety and to purchase emergency phone units throughout the community to make hiking trails safer. Each October, the group sponsored Ella's Run, an event named after Meredith's dog, at a popular trail in Metro Atlanta where Meredith and Ella would go to walk. The festival atmosphere, complete with raffles, food, a 5K run, and a one-mile walk, was a great time. Just like Meredith, her friends are wonderful.

Meredith's grandmother would make the trip from Charleston, South Carolina, and I would walk with her in the one-mile walk as the 5K runners did their thing. I visited with Meredith's friends who had helped search for her back on Blood Mountain. As the years moved on, fewer people recognized me from all the TV press releases back then, which was fine with me. I would say goodbye to Julia and leave soon after the walk. It was always a great event, but it brought back so many memories I was trying to forget. But, over the ten years of the event, I only missed one.

On October 21, 2017, Right to Hike would host Ella's Run for the tenth and final time. I got there early and was greeted by Julia and many other folks I remembered seeing at Vogel State Park during those days in January years ago. Meredith's grandmother was there, but was not able to walk with me this time. I walked alone thinking how much Meredith and Ella must have enjoyed these trails. Dogs of all shapes and sizes seemed to want to run rather than walk with their owners. So they did. Julia recognized several people who had worked hard over the years to sponsor the event. They were presented with a special gift thanking them for their service. I was honored as they presented me with one too. Everyone there urged each other to continue to think about Meredith even though Ella's Run was officially over.

# 17

## THE DREAMS

*Listen, I told you there is no way I can make it on the outside. I've told you before. I'd have to turn around and walk right back in here.*

—Gary Michael Hilton

I was seventeen when I worked my summer job at the decommissioned nuclear laboratory site, and twenty-one when I taught at my old high school. I turned twenty-four not long after joining the GBI. At fifty-nine, I hung up the badge. Now I'm sixty-five. The years went by fast, and now I'm right back where I started. I teach in the Department of Criminal Justice at a small university in the mountains of North Georgia, not far from Blood Mountain. My classes mainly focus on criminal investigations, and I use many of my experiences at GBI as a guide. I reach back in time and tell the students about Marty Zon and our trips working undercover. I tell them about those long nights on the fugitive squad in Atlanta and how lucky I was to survive. The general crime cases I worked gave me an opportunity to teach them about basic criminal investigations like burglary, robbery, and theft. And I tell them about Meredith's case. Most are too young to remember, as back then they were in elementary school, but it's a chance for them to see how things can go.

In the spring of 2008, I was asked to present to the Georgia Emergency Management Agency at their annual convention. They wanted to focus on our successes in the investigation of the murder of Meredith Emerson. I could not, however, do a presentation without focusing on the things that went wrong: The failure of Wachovia to provide us with the information about the ATM attempts. The failure of John Taber to call the tip line right after he talked to Hilton. And why I didn't think to look in Dawson Forest that Thursday night. I was only about three miles away from having a chance to rescue Meredith. But I didn't.

As the years moved on, I was asked to present this case at other law enforcement conferences in the Southeast. I was hoping that teaching others about this case and how it unfolded would somehow help me move on. At first, I think it did. But the dreams keep returning.

The dream is always the same. I don't go to my cabin that night; I go to Dawson Forest. As I drive down Shoal Creek Road past my old summer job site, my car lights illuminate a white van parked on a side road. Gary Hilton is standing outside the van, and as I approach him, he lunges with a knife. I fire my gun and strike Hilton in the face. I keep firing until he falls dead at the campsite. I open the sliding door of Hilton's van, and there she is. Meredith Hope Emerson is scared, injured, but alive. I rush her to the hospital, where she's reunited with her family and friends. At this point, I always wake up and realize it was just a dream. Just a dream.

There are evil people in this world, and Gary Hilton is one of them. Thank goodness most folks will never encounter people like him. That day on Blood Mountain, Meredith Emerson did. But the good overshadowed evil as hundreds of volunteers, who didn't even know Meredith, came together to look for her. Her family and friends were strong and didn't let this monster's actions consume them. The media and police worked together, for a change, as they pushed information to the public during those makeshift press releases at Vogel.

As I look back on those days in January, I want to remember the good in many people, not the evil in one. Oh, I guess I'll still wake up at night thinking about Meredith and wishing I could have known her in life rather than in death. And I also will wonder if we could have done more back then to save her. But I do believe we saved others by arresting Gary Hilton, who soon will have a date with the executioner.

Over the years, I have had many police officers who knew about this case tell me, "That was a good case to retire on."

If they only knew.

# ABOUT THE AUTHOR

John Cagle grew up in a small town in North Georgia. He returned after college to teach in his hometown high school. After a few years, and after his interest in law enforcement grew, he joined the Georgia Bureau of Investigation as a special agent. He rose through the ranks and in 2008 retired as the Special Agent in Charge (SAC) of an investigative field office. After retiring, he went to work as the commander of the investigative division of a local sheriff's office, and later became the chief deputy sheriff. He worked thirty-six years as a criminal investigator.

He is now an adjunct professor in the Department of Criminal Justice at the University of North Georgia and teaches courses in criminal investigation.

He lives in a cabin on top of a mountain in North Georgia and enjoys spending time with his grandchildren, including his youngest granddaughter, whose name is Emerson.

# Other Books by
# John Cagle

*Write to Protect and Serve:*
*A Practical Guide for Writing Better Police Reports*